Introduction

Hi there.

So, you're thinking of starting a traditional window cleaning business? That's great. This book is a good start to give you an insight into the job and what it consists of.

Throughout this book, I will be covering the basics what you will need to get started, which, in turn, will give you a good platform.

Chapter 1
Initial set-up

The initial set-up of buying the kit needed, is fairly cheap, (compared to most businesses) which I will go into on the next few pages. Great rewards will come from it throughout time.

Of course, before you start your business, you need to make sure you have a reliable vehicle as you will need this to store your kit throughout the day, and of course, get to your customers.

CONCLUSION

The mystery and fascination of Bigfoot has persisted through the ages. Although several reports of Bigfoot sightings exist, neither a living nor a dead specimen has given proof of the creature's existence. As Bigfoot sightings are rare events and are only witnessed by individuals or small groups of people at a time, a large portion of the human population considers Bigfoot sightings to be mere hallucinations. Therefore, you could assume that the chief motivation for bringing in a dead Bigfoot specimen may simply be for the Bigfoot believers to say simply, 'Ha, ha, I told you so!' The advocates for bringing in a dead Bigfoot justify their intentions by stating that through an analysis of the dead body, preventative measures can be taken to ensure that this species does not become extinct. Nevertheless, other questions remain unanswered:

- Are we sure that an analysis of the dead body will guarantee protection of the species?
- Is humanity willing to accept a reduction of their individual freedoms and liberties to (perhaps) repopulate the earth with Bigfoot creatures?

The second question may seem a bit scary. First of all, we have become quite accustomed to our current lifestyles, and asking us to restrict our happiness so that an animal species may flourish would almost certainly be met with disapproval. Secondly, if Bigfoot creatures were allowed to flourish, they may endanger humans. Of course, weapons and safe zones (that is, cities) give us some protection from animals, but a Bigfoot would have a pronounced advantage if it decided to attack an unarmed human in the wild. Finally, if the Bigfoot species were to grow to large numbers, I am sure that a hunting season would open for them, as it has for practically every other animal, to keep their population under control.

The final point that I wish to express is that I have written this work without the intention of taking a committed stand on this issue. My only intention was to present both the positive and negative aspects of each view.

Essential Tools

You need to ensure you have the essential tools in order to run your business effectively.

A pair of ladders
Window cleaning bucket
Scrims
Microfibre cloths
Bucket on a belt
Window cleaning mop
Window cleaning blade
Pouches
Sturdy roof rack

A professional kit can cost around £500, for this price you can be assured you will be getting the best products. There is plenty of websites and DIY shops where you can find everything you need, but of course, you need to ensure you are buying high quality products, not the cheap ones as these will not do the job effectively. In time, you'll find yourself spending more money overtime.

The brand I use the most, which is also my personal favourite is Unger. I use this brand, (along with most other window cleaners) because they are reliable and are high quality products (which saves money!).
Using this brand also assures me that I am giving my customers the best services possible.

Mop

A mop is used for cleaning the window and getting any dirt off of it.

Blade

A blade is used after the window has been cleaned with the mop. This is to get any excess water off the window.

Bucket

A window cleaning bucket is used to carry your water for your mop.

Bucket on a belt
This is used to carry your mop around your waist.

Scrims
These are used to dry the window after it has been bladed. These are a little expensive but last a long time. Cheaper brands fray after only a few washes. If you buy pre washed this will save you a lot of time and messing about.

Microfibre cloths

These are used for wet cloths, which is used to wipe the seals and cills to ensure all excess water is cleaned up.

Pouches

These are used to put around your waist to carry your cloths to your customers houses.

Ladders

I recommend a 25ft ladder, this is to ensure you are able to clean the higher windows.

You may want a step ladder for some downstairs windows which you may not need your bigger ladders for.

Roof rack

Quite simple, this for your ladder. You need to ensure you buy the correct one for your car and it is sturdy and safe.

Chapter 2
Traditional Cleaning

In this chapter we will cover "why traditional?" and what it really means.

Traditional window cleaning is the way that people have been cleaning windows for the past 50 years or so, before the water fed pole system came around.

The older generation prefer the traditional way of cleaning. As they say, "it works so why change something that's not broken?"

A lot of window cleaners are now using the water fed pole system.
They're expensive, take up a lot of room, and you can't really see where you're cleaning.

I bought a water fed pole system just to test them, to see why other window cleaners use them. Just like my customers, I found that they leave water marks on the window and overall doesn't clean windows like the traditional way does.

In conclusion, if you want happy and loyal customers, stick with the traditional way.

I like to think that in time, we will see more traditional window cleaners around as there really isn't any better way to do the job than this way.

Over the past few years I have picked up a lot more work from new customers as they don't like the way pole systems clean their windows.

Chapter 3
Advertising

Advertise, advertise, advertise! I can't stress enough how important it is to advertise your business and get your name out there. You need to ensure you advertise as soon as you set up so you can get customers right from the start. The more people who know about you and your business, the more customers you will bring in.

Naming your business
The key to success

Naming your business is one of the most important things you'll do. You need to spend a lot of time ensuring you find the perfect name. Focus on what you do, so customers can see who you are. Don't make the name too complicated as people won't be able to remember you, also they are able to recommend you to potential customers if they remember your name.

Flyers

These are a good way to start, they don't cost a lot of money to make and you can place them in shops as well as post them through the doors of the areas you want to clean.

If you plan to make flyers, you need to ensure they are eye catching but not overloaded with information, otherwise the public will throw them in the bin without looking at them.

You may want to ask your local shop if you can put a poster in their window. This is another good way of attracting customers. The shop keeper may want a fee to do this, or, if you are friendly with them you could offer a discount on their windows instead.

Social Media

Social media is a fantastic way of getting your business out there, everybody uses it so you're bound to find potential customers. Advertise your business on local selling pages and the areas you cover, this way potential customers may get in contact with you if the area they're based is listed.

Set yourself a page up on social media and ask your customers to 'like it' and stay active on the page so it brings in potential customers.

One thing I will not advise is knocking on doors advertising what you do, I am not saying this doesn't work, I'm saying people don't appreciate unexpected callers.

As you can see, there's lots of ways to advertise to get your name out there. You may in time, find other ways which work for you but these are just a few to get you started.

Chapter 4
Keeping track

Keeping track of your work is important so you know where you're at everyday.

You need to ask each customer when they'd like their windows cleaned, most prefer them done every fortnight or once a month.

By knowing this you will be able to keep track of when they're due to be cleaned.

I have kept it simple and straightforward, keeping my work logged with pen and paper. I have made a spreadsheet so I know exactly where I am. I mark down the date the windows have been cleaned with the street name and number, simple as that!

I also have a workbook which I take with me everyday, this has every customer which is due to have their windows cleaned that day. I will write this up at the end of each week ready for the next week.

If you prefer to track your work on your computer there is lots of different spreadsheets to download, or you can make your own.

If you choose to use this method, ensure you save and back up your work to minimise the risk of losing everything if something is to go wrong with the computer.

Price your work on how much you want for your time. Keep it simple, charge by the size of the house. Smaller houses, charge less, bigger houses, charge more.

The day before you are due to clean your customers windows, sending them a text message or email is a good reminder to let them know that their windows are due. I find my customers appreciate this as they can then arrange with me how they're going to pay if they're not going to be home so they don't owe me anything.

This is also a good way to keep contact with your customers to show your ongoing appreciation of their custom.